THE

FALLING

OR

T
E
R
R
A
N
C
E

DOWN

C
E

DANCE

For the brotherhood
of everything Atticus

THE

FALLING

DOWN

DANCE

Chris Martin

COFFEE HOUSE PRESS
MINNEAPOLIS
2015

COVER + BOOK DESIGN by Mary Austin Speaker

COVER ART © Simon Evans and Sarah Lannan

AUTHOR PHOTO © Mary Austin Speaker

Coffee House Press books are available to the trade through our primary distributor, Consortium Book Sales & Distribution, cbsd.com or (800) 283-3572. For personal orders, catalogs, or other information, write to: info@coffeehousepress.org.

Coffee House Press is a nonprofit literary publishing house. Support from private foundations, corporate giving programs, government programs, and generous individuals helps make the publication of our books possible. We gratefully acknowledge their support in detail in the back of this book.

LIBRARY OF CONGRESS CATALOGING-IN-PUBLICATION DATA

Martin, Chris, 1977 August 11-
[Poems. Selections]
The falling down dance / Chris Martin.
pages cm
ISBN 978-1-56689-422-7
1. Experimental poetry. I. Title.

PS3613.A77785F35 2015
811'.6--dc23
2015010592

PRINTED IN THE UNITED STATES

FIRST EDITION | FIRST PRINTING

for Mary Austin Speaker

for Atticus Marker

CONTENTS

Everything between time

PHILIP WHALEN

Time is always something else

ROBERT CREELEY

Time

The last star.

The oldest living insect.

The first bloody lip.

Then we fall asleep

under the rotting walnut tree

in the hopelessly sloped

backyard of the oldest house

in town. It starts over. Falling

temperatures. Runaway

slaves in the earthen basement.

The James Gang drinking in

the living room. Cathy

Wagner living in the attic.

Then the big black ghost dog

was exorcized. The kitchen

wall fell into the garden.

We met the oldest jackrabbit.

Stepped over the oldest blade

of bluegrass. Then Atticus.

The first raspberry.

The last train to nowhere.

Blaring back pain.

Plan where the first step

is falling apart. The oldest water

dropping from a ravaged sky.

Then he discovers his toes.

Then night comes on

with its throb

of platelets. Last word.

First coronation. The sun

was there all along.

The last time

he felt the whole

universe was wet

and inside him.

A man you'll never

meet fells

the world's

oldest tree

and it becomes

tragedy

almanac

timber

house

fire

ash

Hunger

October's

a beautiful time to hover

on the low tilt

of a regional jet on

its trembling

way from Iowa

to Illinois. October

fourth. I

lean against my stranger.

Willow, you green

mammoth. I listen

to Gwendolyn

Brooks address

her abortions. Rotten

broccoli trees, just

gorgeous this time of year.

After we touch

down, next morning, we get October

sunburns in Transmitter

Park, pregnant

hipsters tanning elastic

rounds. The East

River Ferry goes both

ways, graffiti

accuses: YOU WOULD. First

our child was a raspberry,

then a prune, a peach, a fist, now

I fear the metaphors

have stopped. Little plural

urchin. Karaoke October I couldn't

help bassing out

on Love

Will Tear Us Apart.

Never a pear's misshapen and mottled

green. A grape, blackberry

bursting to mango. Skin giving

way to the dawn

of the body. In my heart

I named him Cúchulainn.

In an October of politics

I heard Brooks

obliterate it. Warp

spasm of a ripe belly

and its curling

prawn. I lean against

my stranger, my worker

and singer that handles

the air. I eat at

hearsay, that lank

and wary fruit

until it spells *rupture*.

Carving out

a chamber for the garbled

sun to sing. Entrunk

a fat module.

Trunking a wet life.

Glutted and guessing

this epoch that

like a hiccup weds

us to syncope.

The falling down dance.

The dance gorse

accords the sky, the sky

that dances

in a dog's belly.

A chamber of no foxing

the web. A topaz

grocery we want to own.

In this, our town, we flood

the streets with willow

you green mammoth.

We eat everything.

We tear the weather

apart like meat

with our teeth. Gobbling

flux. An ear

so large and empty

it feels

like a planet stomach.

Regional. October. Gwendolyn. I

seize how

our hidden sun feeds

memory and

lean.

Time

Skyish.

Not air, but

arguing

with chemicals.

Like a drug

made from the span of Set

Adrift

on Memory

Bliss between the first

processed

harmony and the moment the

breakbeat caves

to sample.

Skyish like, I never

don't hear it. *Baby*

you send me. Boring

through the Earth

just as dawn on

one side floats dusk

to the other. Like it's cool

turning Bonita

Applebum into Christina

Applegate, sampling

Spandau Ballet, a joke

for the throes of the executed

during WWII. Baby you

send me. Reminds me

of, *duh*, that kind

of drug. Like it's only time

before Joy Division becomes

Blackwater. But for now

I love this drug.

I keep it on tab

like a leaf inside my lobe.

A fleer echo. I get set

like a crumped chit

wiving

wind. Skyish. Dancing

in the pale orange

cloak of smoke bombs.

It's that

moment when war

becomes leisure. The top

comment on YouTube reads

"I don't know why but when

I listen to this song I wanna fire

my bored employees."

Dawnt. Eely.

Cloudeder.

Oud oud oud.

Economics

Today the whole

cosmos aligns in gossip

like light isn't

ingots only

for speed of seeing

and oppositely the waterfall

of our faces makes

the slowest crystal drop.

A too-curious tick

swims to death in my coffee.

Nature

is truly awful.

All that melted gold

spanked roses

on our cataract. So

of course I hear T-Boz

singing *don't* on my shoulder

offset by Left-Eye's

condom lens like

leaves are prophylactic, each

green-veined jimmy hat

engorging with gold.

Who was the third?

The C. So beautiful and

boring. Blanked.

And thus is name torn from

the heart of ornament.

Nature is truly awful.

Night. The dark. How

does it comprehend

light? Photons pouring

gold into the fathomless

vault. This world is so money.

Like how I texted you a picture

of the wild horse gnawing lawn

outside our hotel window.

Wild and pregnant, on an island

made of target practice. Just

munching away. Bursting

with money.

Time

In the underlit kitchen

where I feel myself gather

like mercury

a sense of evil, cinematic

flowering, following

the denial of the multiple within

and calling that a person

I'm only

making coffee. It's December

in the year of the cicada. Exoskeletal

song of collapse and expansion. The year

our unreadiness took root

and budded true

joy, threaded at all times

by the fear of meaning. I mean

we had a baby. We named him after

a lawyer. 7:14 a.m. and sun just

coming up over the trees

and dusted roofs to rest

on the igloo of the Chrysler

Concorde, sculpture we've come

to accept. Twenty-eight below. The sun's curved

blade feels limp against the wind.

In the other room you're

drinking milk, you're giving milk, my

two yous. And given the blizzard

I can see how it's also the year of that eerie

blank animal

liquid: ukulele milk, boredom

milk, milk

of the taxi cab and milk of

the hermit crab. Radiator milk, Netflix

milk, milk of a thousand downloads

and broken health care. Free

milk of hospitality, milk of the neighborhoods

we can't or won't

afford, and endless milk

of sun melting snow, sending all that white

back to heaven, leaving us

to slosh through clear, cold puddles.

Drinking and giving, sleeping

and crying. Black milk

of the Meters LP teaching you

the beat, how to bounce, so maybe milk

is time after all, intravenous

drip keeping this troubled

sapience apace

in the year of Frank

Ocean. So much

father's milk I feel like an empty truck.

Each week I erase more

milky stalagmites from behind

the nursery curtains, grown

thick against a bitter

freeze, but little Atticus

throbs with brown fat, globby

ingots known

only to babies and bears, sleepers

who can't shiver. He is poor

but rich in proton leaks and capillaries, white

gold and brown fat, flush

and rosy on the coldest of nights

in the year of foreclosure. Steady milk of Jay

Rock's verse on Money

Trees. Milk

of composure, of despair.

The year of trying

to be

at the very least

competent.

Ethics

I sit where I at.

I ask you to work

backward

from start to star

wanting the plosive

to go nova.

We stutter together

fists on the ripcord

until death is a thread

we follow and knot.

Sun stroked and likewise

we awe and crow

at the flaw we make

in the crowd, a busy nest

that samples anesthesia.

We quickly unfold

our numb bundle

to glow and flog

all that's surgical

toward liturgy.

The spell is spelling.

The art in earth.

The if in life.

Without the world

we find each word

winnowed, the egg

in its nest compressed

to a cold seed riven

by ambivalent *or.*

A knot not saying

life. Knock-knock

nest knuckle. Rapping

acme spot. Let us wake

from this bed of bedazzled

leaves, from the depths

of our own grizzly sleep.

Let us slowly emerge

from the text's exit

wound. Rewound.

The scrambled story

inside everything

we destroy. From

the very star.

Time

Let's say you're

a man, a man

who likes looking

at men, a woman, a

woman who likes

looking at men, at

women, a man who

likes looking at

women, necessarily

each and a stranger

walks by in a flower

print, in thick stripes

and worn denim, barefoot

and sleepy, in heavy

boots, in a loose and torn

shirt, a skinny

tie, tortoise shell

sunglasses, in a snug pair

of corduroy shorts, studded

wristband, shaved

smooth, a brown waterfall

of curls, arm sleeved in deep ink

and cuffs rolled up, unreasonably

tall, possessing almost

antiquely small hands, wearing

a necklace made of shells and trailing

the scent of cut wood, this stranger

squirming past, solidly

striding out of view, and in the impossible

dilation of this moment you are

caught

in the existing of a person

who moves

across rooms. The it

that was you

tugged into the throe

of parenthesis.

You die. What's its name?

It doesn't have one. It's

wave. Borne. A magnet. The leash

off and a vacuum

of (you) roves. Unperform.

Song

I wake thinking like a manifold

of dim animals, autobiological, a blood highway

thanking light

for its unseen horizon, as daily

Adamic *logos*

slowly pushes its smug

slithering way through the soft

tissue of my gums. By which

I mean the problem

with language is its compulsive

replacement

of song. I hear Atticus

rip open

morning's doors

with his wail, crib animal

ripping pitch

to know difference, the slip

where one tone

becomes its other, restless

and necessary

fragments of a song

so old only the youngest

singers get it, flooding

chamber and light

coursing through the leafless

city trees, through power

lines, orange-pink toward

a blue west where

the ear grows

its tiny garden of fear, cluster

of doubt flowers courting the blossom

of language. So a baby's

a boombox, right? Cutting

teeth from pop

to talk radio. I wake and then

I wake and then the I woke

broke for both wanting

to pay ourselves for raising the baby.

He says tuh tuh tuh, damp

match of each plosive

striking against a still

moving tooth, deciduous, ridged milk

leaf that quakes, cuts, and erupts.

I don't want him to give up

song for word's currency

but, you know, I need to speak

with him. He sticks his

hand inside the jewelry box

of my mouth, roughly

cataloguing each pale facet. For him

that's just the news, a moment

before animal after animal spools

loose. He says da da da, dental

occlusive meaning he's ready

to surface from the open and mournful

weather of the vowel, make transit

from song to speech, from spirit

to society, cutting teeth

toward apples and waging light

against the mouth's wet

and glottal cave. I woke without

knowing how I work

or works, without

words, after and before

the baby, who had just nursed

back to sleep. I woke because

I love being halfway

between dream and day, song

and talk, still unsteady

as morning's escort, that blurred

ferry of cortical longing,

carries us to where

we pay with consciousness.

From here you can watch

every wounded

animal of thought lurk

and convalesce

on the other shore, stalking

in peripatetic glyphs, desire

always and already

dance. I woke and wrote to slow

this convalescence, animal

I would not see

annihilated, wrote

from within animal folds, folds

I stole from the baby, autonomic

and naming each beast

before it could disappear, the horizon

where autobiology turns

autoimmune, attacking the self

that it doesn't

understand. Atticus remained

asleep, finally, his tooth

soothed by Mary's milk's analgesic

surge. His others, his animals,

safely intact, song

before talking and dance before

walking. The sky is pink

before it's blue and black before

that. Now it's 7:18 a.m. and I

subjugate the sky

by language, like Adam

did the beasts, a book

that wants to break

the unwieldy

noun back down

to a time

when it was still

creeping. I'm awake

now no longer

stumbling with song, and find myself

walking the far shore, thanking

and naming, wondering

how much more there would be

to sing if we

could only stop

talking.

Time

What

if these were

notes not

for something more

finished, but for something more

like ruins, not Gothic

Revival Horace

Walpole fakes, not stonewashed

jeans, but real ruins, lived-in almost

to death, a little ruin

of a typewriter that bit rib-

bon ribbon ribbon

until each blackened tooth

smashed, guiding a whole polis

toward spoil, and say

these ruins weren't like other ruins

in that they were invisible

to commodity, no one

would ever stand in front of them

in a photograph, or rub

one of their crumbly faces

into ghost, or point

at a dot near the crease of a cheap

map, but ruins only accessible

by stumble, a ruin you come

upon like someone else's

life left

between a stand

of hairy pines no one thought

to walk through again, it wasn't

a way anyone actually going

somewhere would go, a huge fucking

mess, and now it's just

this nothing

pointing

everywhere but at itself, this event

you (now) and only now (you)

are allowed to see, a tragedy

that barely even unfolds, trembles

like a river that

never seen never

moves, and can't be

an event

because there aren't any streets

to walk home on, string

to ravel, there's only

this ruin running

in place, a Brigadoon tricking

us into missing something

else, everything, some fat

animal staring at reason, a bear

furrowing, and this ruin, this impossible

strip of "life" will

drift with other endless parts

of you you lost

along the way, over all

this time, will shift

and disappear like another

gleaming doorknob, will shift

and disappear like

Memory

Now and now and now

at the Buttermilk, vast

forest yawns open beside

the line for the bathroom

deciding the F is

for flinch over Pathmark

when our car suddenly

floods with sun. In other

words, the G just left and won't

return, crossing Atlantic's

Dead Marshes, wan

arms of flattened commuters

groping our ankles. We list

the singles keeping us

up at night. Mine's

I don't want to explain I want

to get high. The roof spilling

us over its tar edge. Bed

cigarette crooning with a stray

dog chorus into the wrong

window from no-man's-land.

The S never curves. It's where

all these buildings run out

of money. Forever helicopter.

Saving and condemning. Late

subway hand caked with rubber.

Mac, your girlfriend's missing

finger is still at Freddy's, deep

beneath the Jay-Z concert

at Barclay's Center. We meet

at O'Conner's, take the Q

everywhere. No one tells

us how to go home

so we don't. We share loosies

by the barbed wire banks

of the Gowanus where the barge

says I love you. I leave you

cab money and you get your head

stapled. Hang on. Styrofoam

at the Turkey's Nest and tackling

dummies of broken glass.

A dollop of cold Prospect

ice cream in your sister's eye.

It's impossible to find

Basquiat's grave, but Psycho

plays on repeat in the chapel

as we toss watermelon

rinds into the curling roof gape

of the burnt-out factory.

Wine is for late last spattering

stoop, tongue, I turn

on Washington, find the lone

open bodega, buy Dunhill

reds and return. This crosswalk

green means *run*. We stroke

the sensor and spill on.

Paperbag it at the church.

Double churro on the N.

Our livers our police.

I guess it's about time

we get these teeth right.

Boss on the jukebox.

Thunder Road, 16th St.

We get it already, the train

is an apartment.

Time

Snow is the conversation

winter makes with itself. No

quarrel, just endless

pretty tedium, blank

babble, the baby

making his thizz face

with a fistful

of white melting against

his quartet of teeth.

I want and write

myself here

for and with

you because

that's what I really

want, company.

The same as

saying desire is desire

to enfold, layer, imbricate, a word

I'm sure is right, though

at this hour I can't

recall what it means: to shingle

voices like a Spanish roof.

Here in the itchy

insect darkness

my synapses grind

and spark like the car

I hear starting up

on the near-arctic street

or the baby's plush

pajamas, crackling

static electricity and sudden

light as I enter his blacked-out

room, the moment

after he's cried his first cry

of the day. All winter the snows

come, often at night.

Late February and now

the pale fin at the tip

of the plastic Adirondack

beneath the barren pear tree

is all that remains

exposed, our dying yard shark.

First Atticus was a piglet,

snuffling hungry, a sloth

almost impossible

to wake, a stumble ape

and a dolphin and lately

he's been the pigeon

we let coo until the blue

bruise of morning emerges

beneath the curtain.

Or maybe that was me.

Atticus is screaming.

Braying, growling, always

moving with sharklike persistence

even in sleep, even while feeding

his arms flap and his eyes

roll, his feet kick

and his mouth breaks

into smile or desperation.

Beached pink nurse

shark, bald and toothy, talking

to the wall or thrashing

against the nibbled bars.

At six o'clock we relent.

I turn the doorknob,

turn on the light. He's face

down in the basin

of his parched white

and slatted sea

and when I turn him over

he's so happy to see me he's

shaking.

Music

You put the needle

on the record. You put

your tongue against the beach

where our teeth meet

a sea of gums. You say

tongue. We say *stay.* You put

the needle on

the record and think

into the morning snow

that fills a tree's inverted

crotch. It's winter.

These thoughts are soon

indistinguishable

from the new snow now

fallen. You put

the needle on the

record, but we hear

inextinguishable, as if the needle

skipped, as if this snow

is a fire, whitest

clump of January flame.

You put the needle

on the record and think

Sex in Winter. It falls

in flaming clumps

the shovel of your mind can pile

into colorless wheelbarrows

of pulse and nerve.

We put on our hat and gloves.

You tuck your shirt

into your long underwear.

We fuck all winter.

You put the needle

on the record and it burns

far whiter than a blank

page, far whiter than even

the word *sclera*. We look deep

into the tree and say

sclera. Say *now*. The flame

licks your brain. Your thoughts

fall to where the tree meets

the buried lawn. Truest

yellow music. Winter song and exit

sex. New high thaw. You put

the needle on the record and the last

thing you do before

we fuck is think about us

fucking.

Time

Among many tongues may clang

the bell of ten thousand names.

A clepsydra with veins of blood.

A caravel on a tide of bloodletting

is also our necessary clock, so

the he who is I at the

time lets out my elephantine toll.

Vein of granite, vein of quartz.

Piezoelectric hum wherefore

we cast a tiny ear of water, we

who clang and unmoor our fleet.

Education

Snuffle

pig. Creaky pink

door. Crumblefoot.

Chubbery bean. Gurgler.

And Paul says, the very thing

that would destroy a fish

is its desire to graze

on the hills like sheep.

When I pick you up

your eyes go agog

startled and smiling

and nowhere

are our animals more

evident. I rest you manifold

in the hollow of my palm

and now here

I am standing on the other

side of death, throat

open as a singing door, you

the one who puts us

here, here, the grounding where

I fear not life and love

the living.

Time

The present is taking part

of the landscape

to heart, its *ands,* those sudden

additions fording

nothing

to make the world

world. Heat

rash spattering his pallid

cheek. Cold white stove in

the rented kitchen.

Four crows on a minivan

with three flat tires.

I went back to the beginning

note, the stalled burst

of fanfare

that turns what's

ordinary

spectacular. Cat's paw

on the centipede. Stills

from a movie

no one's watching.

We want the dawn

of acknowledgment

wildfiring

the baby's face to spill

and spread into the floorboards

and doorknobs. To turn

the job

of the object, its fisted

thinging

miraculous, while each

and adds up

and despite it.

Tilling. Tilting

the field one anticipates

into the verse

one doesn't. Now

until whatever else adds

itself, resemblance

over the break. Click

save. Take

this bouquet of fingers.

Wait. Tick skewered

by a pink thumbtack.

Wet red flower.

Language

Raining, morning, reckoning, what else

has it been

so endless

a question we

as state can state

plainly. So why

the embellishment, the body

breaking

bullish and red

into alien blossom?

Another pedunculated

balloon in the cave

of my armpit, little blush

I welcome among the whorls.

I remember the first time

I saw the cherry blot

beneath my eye, how

long had it been

glowing and soldered

there? The doctor

called it a spider

angioma, vascular web

radiating harmless

tumors. Charmless humor

of the body budding

out, a compulsion to rhyme cell

with cell. John Clare

on his way to the asylum.

So this morning it rained the moment

I woke, Atticus sleep-eating, all of Pleasant

Avenue simple with the pavement going

from light to dark gray. Plainly.

I drank light

brown coffee, embellished

by whole milk and coarse sugar.

A day. Plainly. Body

starved for the good news

of weather. Primeval hand painting

the sidewalk a new hue.

I wanted to tell you something

about the shipwreck

of fatherhood, of motherhood, the coarse

sugar leaving us

shook. Soft wreck of the baby

greeting each kiss

with an open

and drooling mouth, reflex

we don't understand.

We song

all day, breaking

in and out

milk

and sleep, eye

filled

with flinches, asteroid

curd of it

half-digested

on the sleeve. Hoping

for a nervous breakthrough.

Love and love's opposite

which is not hate but despair

threaten and then do,

they capsize

us all day long. Now

it's evening and the lakes

are black in the sky.

Disjecta, an estate sale, the filleted

wreck of time

rhyming

with history. Does the baby think

it's wrong? Does the very word

man strike him as just

another strange humiliation?

And who knew the eggplant

had thorns?

But let's be honest

it's my birthday, awash

in the immense

and candied tedium of being

Dad. The New York Times

tells me August 11th is significant

for being the day least

likely for someone to type

depression

into a search window. Home

in the galaxy. Desiring

facile silence

from what's necessary. We rise

on the wings of pain

to greet a terrifying sea

that can't stop

laughing.

Plain as that.

We can't stop laughing.

John Clare

rhyming thicket

with hiccup

as the manifold

animal

of the baby tumbles out.

There's no such thing

as a breakdown, death,

or asylum.

We can't stop

Time

I say the sun

is a portal and also

the cutout

vestment of a feeling for going

on. Ticketless, morning

metes

out its open

hour, melted green

hush only just

slightly

upset by the occasional

arriving

jet, like back pay.

Outside, seventeen-year cicadas

fill the air and then

the concrete.

Since Atticus arrived

life couldn't be

more full, more full of, more off, more

effulgent, glut of all things

grown and sown

until our garden won't stop

bursting, as what's

continually new flops

out and open

in the spirit (*numen*)

of Oppen

and his numer-

ousness, now

ours, so that

this bower unraveling

can happily overflow

capsize and grow

lost, as without knowing how

we find new

way each

morning, each sun

novel, loving

unaccountably

the us that unshuts

the door of light, orange

throng, on

on on

Business

Sun chiding glut

of flung dust

discos the bedroom

until my nostrils

are swollen, cold of October's first

day swapping yellow

for green on the maple as you

half-doze, having

woke so

many times to feed

the teething baby, who himself

finally sleeps, his strangely strong arms

raised in mysterious victory.

A gentle mania is all

that goads the day

forward, purple current

of the world

plugging us in. I open

software, drink

coffee, hear

the birds squabble

like toddlers, can they be toddlers?

At 8:17 a.m. there's a moment

of silence that feels entirely

apocalyptic. So these are the notes

of sudden dad stoned on bare

life, rabid and full

a-thrum

before the stupid, torpid, turbid

slog of capital

goes engine, goes

gorgeously off and plods

away our hours. Wealth,

like guns, should be harder

to get, impossible

to keep, and a little more comfort

for everybody. I open a file, save, fly

my tattered potlatch

sail, mare's tails in the sky

twitching

under the anxious weight

of a storm that never

arrives. Or, never

arriving, its false nascent shadow

moves inside, displacing lungs

with money. For now

the baby dreams himself

a full gold head

of hair, but mistypes

it as *hear.* A toddler crashes

into the rain-fresh window, sun

occluded, day occult, glittering spinnaker

of free downloads acting balloon

to commerce. New Drake.

Zombies. The last episode

of Girls. That's

when I find

you're awake, you're

singing the baby

his morning

song: *We're all*

in our faces with

bright shiny places

and this is the way

we start out

our day.

Time

Pronominal despite

having lodged rock after

rock of thought

to block self-light's

gurgling flow, days

envein me.

But listen, it's a

belonging world: each

being busy being

the burr in

another's snarl

a squirrel regards

from the lawn

between properties.

So of course I love

the difficulty

of, not living, but

living *with*

this horde of pulsing

flesh, loci, voice

of everything that spills

from time's swollen

and splitting lip.

Mary, days

overdue, says my mustache

smells like lemongrass.

What we want now

is endless

tentacle fingers to grip

afternoon's tracking

shot as it hits

afternoon's edge, tips

and tumbles into night's

fair warning fringe.

Today I wake larger

in late April's amplified

light and pause to toe

old slats with a torn callus

at the upstairs window

painted shut. Frozen yard

we know is thick

with hidden warrens.

Protracted clench. World

just beginning to blush

against this aging

winter's brace, all except

us, full and throbbing

around the thorn

of thought, this one, this

knowing not

when it will come

or just how, this he, this

togethered, threaded

being, bone

and skin. There

it is, crystal

rearrangement.

Fate is the armor

of flesh.

Home

Now that I live in the land of the mound

effigies I figure

it's time to take the leavings

of my heart and make

a buffalo. Swollen

shuffling Goliath. Matted

russet buffalo pustule. Shag

swarm. A buffalo so

utterly

distended it could only

be pregnant with history.

We put on our hats and take out our knives

and carve the party into fist-sized cubes

of dead red history cake.

Cursive leather frosting that reads

don't come around here

no more. I say

it over and over. I don't

like strangers like

me. I've eaten way

too much party mound

and I think I'm going to be rich.

I get blind and spin with a dissevered animal

tail in the stickled clutch of my palm

until I'm just

rich as fuck and filled

with an unkind wind.

Still, I piss straight

into it and always under

a stranger's stars.

Piss and whistle. Don't come

around here no more. The stars

are so cold

my teeth could

up and shatter. I gather

white dust in my

wallet. I swirl

my teeth in the vacuum

of the sky's unbuyable

until I'm smiling

the Milky Way. I look up

and see the footprint moon

thieving and tiptoeing

through my grin. I can only

stomp and whinny and

in the morning

I eat cigarette apples

and cough the sun black.

Time

All that happens happens

in the hollow

mouth

open mid-vow

knowing

only song will do

what an empty cave needs

done, drone

that seeds to fill

one space and then that

space's space, what

are we made

of if

not chants.

Sun slumping up

the stucco, cat chewing

her tail clean, nimbi

darkening the fallen

leaves leatherlike, I make

voice, voice, voice, voices

like a fist

on thinking's door

a fistula

wrapping abstraction

and binding it to what, morning

sickness, the lathed light

now flying through branches

made sinister

by season, a crook

in our amygdala's gray

ministry and all

I see is a circling murder

above the antenna

that replaced the weathervane.

All I see is one-

millionth

percent of the earth

at once. Chance.

I give you the fingers

of my hand

like I was giving you broken

rulers.

Dance

Sit up, spit up, endless

terror and frontier

of the body unfolding, sun

and bone, bubbling

forth, affront

to all things steady, he thinks

he'll skip

crawling. He's falling.

It's twenty-five below and he's standing

on the radiator, watching

the snow-buried

cars go nowhere, nobody

holding him, it, this

taut body that keeps building

itself like a winter

turnip, keeps

turning milk into the root

of all that's sudden

to lurch past

ecstasy into despair

and back, rapt

radish growing more

red in our half-finished winter

basement. Pause

for a breath people in a hurry

can't feel. It's time

to childproof the sockets, to scrub

black mold from the cracked

wainscot and hide

our copy of After Lorca.

Does he get bigger or does

the world shrink before him? We keep

taking it away. On his

nine-month birthday he eats

bright orange pieces

of shredded cheese, chokes

on a clementine, snow

falling, filling

in the path from the back door

to the garage. It's dropped

to forty below with the

windchill the morning

he finally does it

crawls across

the nursery lured by

a neon monster

pencil top, the kind

you win with skee-ball tickets.

All week we surround

him in the wonky

quadrilateral of our

outstretched legs, feet

touching, forming

the enclosure where he falls

back and forth, you

to me and me

to you. We secretly fear

he likes the falling

down dance so much

he'll never walk, but we love

watching him practice

collapse. Unfolding, bubbling

crawling, falling, standing, watching,

holding, building, turning,

growing, taking, filling,

falling, forming

I there and you here

and the nucleus

of our desires strewn

over the difference, which is now

a person. Let us each lean

and fall soft in this piecemeal field

where we can stumble

and learn freely, forage

song from tragedy, light

from loss, fall

into evening, morning, the next

day, mercy. A person.

Time

Sun through sleet

coppers a bare

and brittle limb

so that underneath

I see it, the sudden

pavement, first

naked corner, exactly

where we stood

yesterday in our boots

and beside it

emerge thawed

clumps of edging sod.

We gather fingers

into a pulse knot

and join the compact

earth, loosening

by dint of what

else, sun. I grab at

your hand, swinging

free, clamor after

moment's—what can

it be called except

amen. Heart-blip stuck

in the radar of my finger

tapping and speeding

memory of yesterday out

the window I'm

pushing barely open

eyes through

and swollen

fingers beating

this down, crowding

the sod with us.

The sleet with us.

The sidewalk, elder

bugs dead and stuck

to the screen, me

on me, on you.

The world we

together. Mary.

All our fingers.

That world.

Art

We leave the frozen

north for the half-frozen

southwest, leave

the driveway, climb

the hill, a December

sun falling behind

the mountain or what passes

for one in this adobe

state, the ghost

white of frigid chamisa

falling everywhere and my eyes

so open

they begin listening

at the periphery, the particulate

air, where they snag

on a pitiful scrub

pine, pulling

its tough green into orbit

around my iris, a color the Romans

called livid. Atticus is strapped

to my chest, his open palm

grazing the desiccated

blossoms, curling closed

around a tuft of piñon

like a starfish

eating a sea urchin. If only

he was as gentle

with the faces of the ones

he loves, who love

him, bloodying

Granddaddy's

lip with the violent joy

of reunion. We repeat this

word over and over,

gentle, but he is a brute

and handles the world

as if nothing

in it could break. Maybe

he's right. Or maybe breaking

open is just what

we do

before whatever

is us is

recapitulated, remedied

a bluebird

whirling low

between pines. It's too fast

for Atticus to track, but we all hear

its call, said to resemble

the word *few*, or maybe *phew!*

I catch the gray

bobbing belly

in my livid eye. *Few*

few, calling

scarcity out, open, the way

its threat belies

an undeniable abundance. We

suddenly see how red-threaded

this world is, tangled, and rereading

the desert's throb

under all that snow, Atticus

is batting at his own

worn red nose, dutiful

thermometer. We reach

the museums on the hill

where common

desire grows

uncommon, flays

compliance to swell

and throb

where the unmanaged

blaze. We take off

our hats and gloves, blessing

the weather that leaves us

bothered, gentle

thanks even the baby

understands. The bracing that gives

way to embrace. The needles

of the pine there

to be touched, and so too

the cold pane, which he gives

a raspberry. I think

I'm beginning

to understand how brute

and livid love doffs

grace only to regain it

bringing new worlds

into orbit, affront

to everything steady.

When we get home he races

around the house, hands

clutching my fingers so tight

the knuckles swell. Then he's calm

and searches the floor for

specks, treasure. We give him

a ribbon, a spoon. Everything is art

to be broken. The cat

and the bowl. Finally he sleeps

in the room with the skylight

blocked by tinfoil, tiny

holes for stars, muted clamor

ripping the night open.

Time

So spitting late and pickled
encomium, I find myself moving
on the verge of a blur
from demotic
to demonic, pink
curling muscle
of tongue flexed and tumescent
against the palette, swollen
as all organs grow and are
monstrous. Tonight
we let him cry. Tomorrow
the ice will liquidate
by noon, by which I mean
I've never been so happy
just to see asphalt, devastated
waiting for light and city
to return, to return in it.
Late March and heavy we lay
listening to him cry
out, not
for hunger but loneliness
forging patch after patch over

each new absence

grown in sleep's now

tattered fabric, pungent

fleece, by which

I mean he's crying and he can't

even squeeze a blanket for fear

he'll suffocate. *Fuck.*

It's late, it's early, it's less

crying than screaming, word-barren

banshee at 12:30, 1:15, 2:50, 5:00,

6:15 and we're up, saggy

bags of face, throbbing relief

and content just

to flop on the carpet, don

our mixing bowls as hats, halos

of acrid urine mist

christening resolve and Atticus

blowing raspberries to the sun.

How many nights go

so punctured, we cease

to know. The snow turns

to water and the water to ice

and the ice to flood. We break

from the chrysalis of still

if still changeable

derangement, we take, tentative

and wobbling, to the streets, shaking

the hands of our neighbors

and wondering aloud how

it's been for them, this Swiss

cheese winter sleep, dingy

and blasted cloth. They speak

and yet it seems

everyone's common

loss remains largely

private, estranged even

(or primarily)

from ourselves, demon

of winter, occult

patience, impatience, winter

stone we pass

each morning as the baby's face

melts and reconstitutes smiling.

There is a lemon in the sky.

Spring comes and instantly

we re-architecture

the cloister of our heart, shower

in the garden, self-diorama

we break open to admit

world. Light

is a sledgehammer.

Juice of real

lemons sketching

the palm's diagram

in pale yellow. Late

March gives way

to early everything and the house

flops inside-out, cave to farm

as the planted crib

is nightly splintered, skinny

leg-stalks breaking

the slats into boyhood.

Who can sleep soundly

in the brazen April blur?

The scream is now

what others call laughing,

spasm built to slake

ice with fire, to rage

fire with wind, a singing

throat coaxes from where

else: heart, stomach. Early

hour and every edge

of the apocalypse is but sprinting

distance away. The crows

are blown from tree to tree

like advertisements

for survival. The sun stays

up past dinner, past bedtime.

In the dark of the morning

we lay unsated, full

awake, listening to world

unfold, our sweet nothing.

ACKNOWLEDGMENTS

This book is deeply indebted to the eyes and ears of Chris
Fischbach, Dan Poppick, Ted Mathys, Joyelle McSweeney,
Mark Levine, Paula Cisewski, Greg Hewett, Jared Stanley,
and Mary Austin Speaker.

I also want to name a few of the many people who have taught
me about care: Mary, Jere and Ron Martin, Courtney Martin,
John Cary, Dana Ward, Sam Gould, Sam Anders, and Ben Polk.

Thank you to my lovely friends Simon Evans and Sarah Lannan
for their original cover art and to Mary once more for her
gorgeous design.

Additional gratitude is owed all the editors who saw early hours
of this book into the world:

Business: *Ampersand Review*, Corey Zeller
Economics: *The Death and Life of Great American Cities*,
    Judah Rubin
Ethics & Home: *Revolver*, Esther Porter
Hunger & Time (sky): *Fence*, Brian Blanchfield, Farid Matuk
    & Rebecca Wolff
Language: *SPOKE TOO SOON*, Kelin Loe & Leora Fridman
Memory: *Brooklyn Rail*, Anselm Berrigan

Music: *Elderly,* Jamie Townsend

Time (ruins): *Wild Horses of Fire,* Thom Donovan

Time (chance) & Time (clock): *Poem-a-Day,* Alex Dimitrov

Time (poison): *Paperbag,* Petro Moysaenko

Time (world): *The Cultural Society,* Zach Barocas

Time (shark): *Where Eagles Dare,* Steve Orth

Time (milk): *Octopus,* Joseph Mains

Time (light): *Kindling Quarterly,* David Michael Perez

And for hours that were left behind:

Apocalypse, Freedom & Faith: *Bombay Gin,* J'Lyn Chapman

Horror & Dance: *Dusie,* Carrie Hunter

Nature: *Sprung Formal,* Jordan Stempleman

Science: *Ghostwriters of Delphi,* Lauren Ireland

Time (fauna), Time (defect) & Time (trapdoor): *The Operating System,* Lynne DeSilva-Johnson

Chris Martin Recommends
These Coffee House Press Books

Null Set, Ted Mathys

The First Flag, Sarah Fox

Body Clock,
Eleni Sikelianos

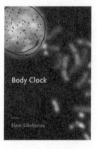

Bright Brave Phenomena,
Amanda Nadelberg

Margaret & Dusty,
Alice Notley

LITERATURE
is not the same thing as
PUBLISHING

Funder Acknowledgments

Coffee House Press is an independent, nonprofit literary publisher. All of our books, including the one in your hands, are made possible through the generous support of grants and donations from corporate giving programs, state and federal support, family foundations, and the many individuals that believe in the transformational power of literature.

We receive major operating support from Amazon, the Bush Foundation, the Jerome Foundation, the McKnight Foundation, Target, and the National Endowment for the Arts. To find out more about how NEA grants impact individuals and communities, visit www.arts.gov. In addition, this activity is made possible by the voters of Minnesota through a Minnesota State Arts Board Operating Support grant, thanks to a legislative appropriation from the arts and cultural heritage fund.

Coffee House Press receives additional support from many anonymous donors; the Alexander Family Foundation; the Archer Bondarenko Munificence Fund; the Elmer L. & Eleanor J. Andersen Foundation; the David & Mary Anderson Family Foundation; the Buuck Family Foundation; the Carolyn Foundation; Dorsey & Whitney Foundation; the Lenfestey Family Foundation; the Mead Witter Foundation; the Schwab Charitable Fund; Schwegman, Lundberg & Woessner, P.A.; Penguin Group; US Bank Foundation; VSA Minnesota for the Metropolitan Regional Arts Council; the Archie D. & Bertha H. Walker Foundation; the Wells Fargo Foundation of Minnesota; and the Woessner Freeman Family Foundation.

The Publisher's Circle
of Coffee House Press

Publisher's Circle members make significant contributions to
Coffee House Press's annual giving campaign. Understanding
that a strong financial base is necessary for the press to meet
the challenges and opportunities that arise each year, this group
plays a crucial part in the success of our mission.

"Coffee House Press believes that American literature should be
as diverse as America itself. Known for consistently championing
authors whose work challenges cultural and aesthetic norms, we
believe their books deserve space in the marketplace of ideas.
Publishing literature has never been an easy business, and
publishing literature that truly takes risks is a cause we believe
is worthy of significant support. We ask you to join us today in
helping to ensure the future of Coffee House Press."
—The Publisher's Circle Members of Coffee House Press

Publisher's Circle members include many anonymous donors,
Mr. & Mrs. Rand L. Alexander, Suzanne Allen, Patricia Beithon,
Bill Berkson & Connie Lewallen, E. Thomas Binger & Rebecca
Rand Fund of the Minneapolis Foundation, Robert & Gail Buuck,
Claire Casey, Louise Copeland, Jane Dalrymple-Hollo, Mary
Ebert & Paul Stembler, Chris Fischbach & Katie Dublinski,
Katharine Freeman, Sally French, Jocelyn Hale & Glenn Miller,
Jeffrey Hom, Kenneth & Susan Kahn, Kenneth Koch Literary
Estate, Stephen & Isabel Keating, Allan & Cinda Kornblum,
Leslie Larson Maheras, Jim & Susan Lenfestey, Sarah Lutman
& Rob Rudolph, Carol & Aaron Mack, Olga & George Mack,
Joshua Mack, Gillian McCain, Mary & Malcolm McDermid, Sjur
Midness & Briar Andresen, Peter Nelson & Jennifer Swenson,
Marc Porter & James Hennessy, the Rehael Fund-Roger Hale &
Nor Hall of the Minneapolis Foundation, Jeffrey Sugerman &
Sarah Schultz, Nan Swid, Patricia Tilton, Stu Wilson & Melissa

Barker, Warren D. Woessner & Iris C. Freeman, and Margaret & Angus Wurtele.

For more information about the Publisher's Circle and other ways to support Coffee House Press books, authors, and activities, please visit www.coffeehousepress.org/support or contact us at: info@coffeehousepress.org.

Typeset in Walbaum and Twentieth Century

Designed by Mary Austin Speaker

Allan Kornblum, 1949–2014

Vision is about looking at the world and seeing not what it is, but what it could be. Allan Kornblum's vision and leadership created Coffee House Press. To celebrate his legacy, every book we publish in 2015 will be in his memory.

Chris Martin is the author of *Becoming Weather* (Coffee House Press, 2011) and *American Music* (Copper Canyon Press, 2007), chosen by C. D. Wright for the Hayden Carruth Award. He is also the author of several chapbooks, including *HISTORY* (Coffee House Press, 2014), *enough* (Ugly Duckling Presse, 2012), and *How to Write a Mistake-ist Poem* (Brave Men, 2011). He is an editor at Futurepoem books and will be a visiting assistant professor at Carleton College in 2016.